Michael Faraday

HE WHO INSPIRED EINSTEIN

Biography of a Scientist Grade 5 |
Children's Biographies

DISSECTED LIVES
auto biographies

First Edition, 2020

Published in the United States by Speedy Publishing LLC, 40 E Main Street, Newark, Delaware 19711 USA.

© 2020 Dissected Lives Books, an imprint of Speedy Publishing LLC

Dissected Lives Books are available at special discounts when purchased in bulk for industrial and sales-promotional use. For details contact our Special Sales Team at Speedy Publishing LLC, 40 E Main Street, Newark, Delaware 19711 USA. Telephone (888) 248-4521 Fax: (210) 519-4043.

10 9 8 7 6 * 5 4 3 2 1

Print Edition: 9781541953796
Digital Edition: 9781541956797

See the world in pictures. Build your knowledge in style.
www.speedypublishing.com

Table of Contents

Michael Faraday's name may not be as common as Albert Einstein's, Thomas Edison's, or Nikola Tesla's, but his contributions to science are immeasurable. In fact, it was Faraday's work that inspired Einstein to make his great discoveries. A chemist and physicist, Faraday's work laid the groundwork for advances in the field of electromagnetism. In this book, we will examine the life, work, and impact of this 19th century English scientist.

Michael Faraday

Early Life

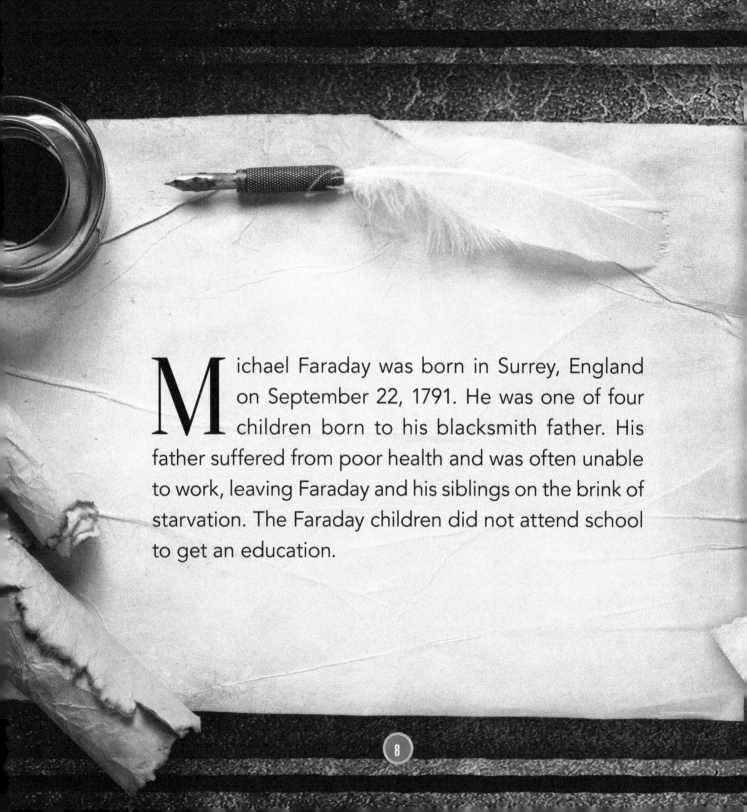

Michael Faraday was born in Surrey, England on September 22, 1791. He was one of four children born to his blacksmith father. His father suffered from poor health and was often unable to work, leaving Faraday and his siblings on the brink of starvation. The Faraday children did not attend school to get an education.

Due to Faraday's father's poor health, he and his siblings were left on the brink of starvation.

Michael noted that he learned to read and write and work basic math sums while attending his church's Sunday school.

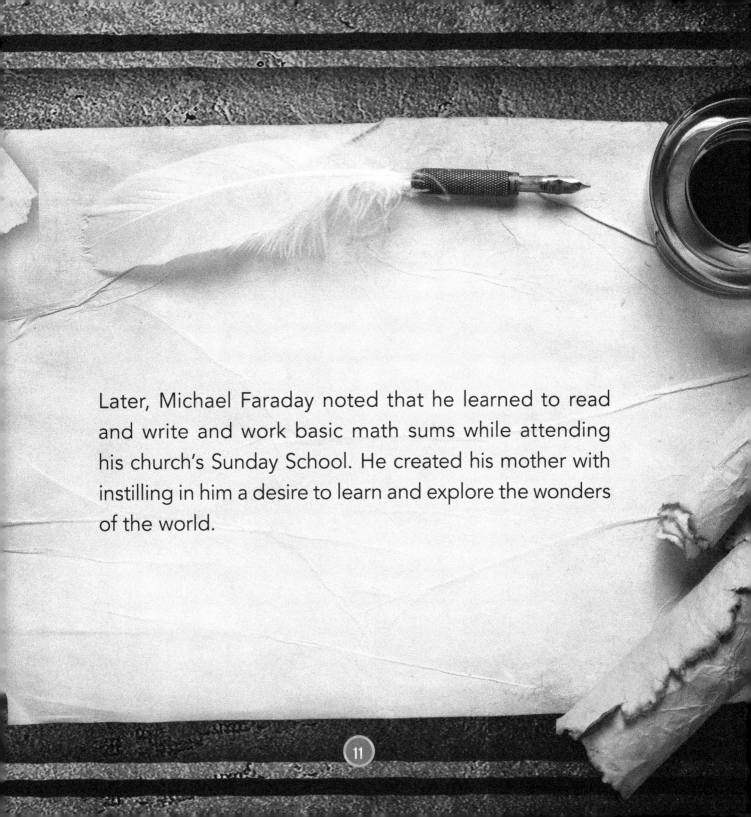

Later, Michael Faraday noted that he learned to read and write and work basic math sums while attending his church's Sunday School. He created his mother with instilling in him a desire to learn and explore the wonders of the world.

Michael Faraday's parents were members of a little-known religious Christian sect[1] that greatly influenced his later scientific observations. In his native England, the group was known as the Sandemanians, but they were adapted from a Scottish order, the Glasites, that was founded by John Glas in the 1730s.

---

[1] Sect – A group following a specific religious belief or doctrine.

John Glas

A doctrine of the Sandemanian belief was to view nature as the creation of God, yet there was an order and process that could be learned. Although there are many people who believe that science and religion cannot co-exist, Faraday's faith was an asset to his scientific endeavors.

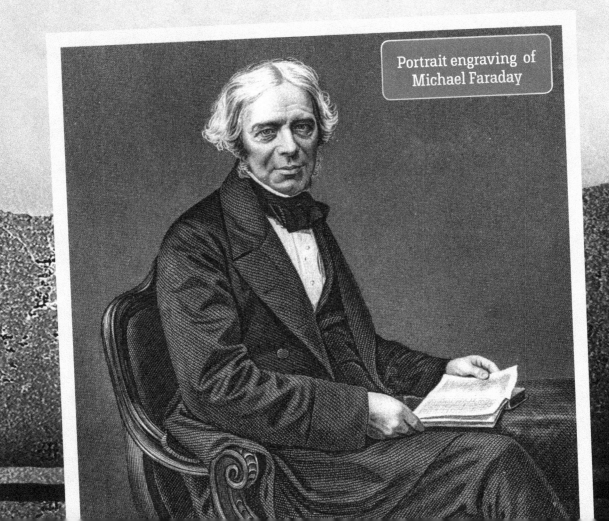

Portrait engraving of Michael Faraday

A Young
Apprentice

As a youngster, Michael Faraday delivered newspapers for a local bookseller to earn extra money for his family. When he turned 14 years old, he became an apprentice[2] to this bookseller, in hopes of learning printmaking and bookbinding skills so he could find a job as an adult.

---

[2] Apprentice – A young teen or adult who works for a craftsman in order to learn the trade.

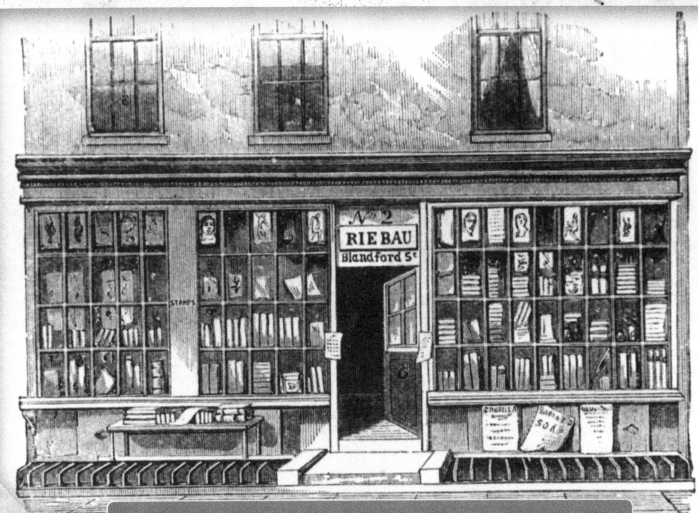

Engraving of Mr Riebau's bookshop at 2 Blandford, London, England, where Michael Faraday worked as an apprentice bookbinder and delivery boy.

Faraday read the books he was working on, which helped to open his eyes to thoughts and ideas of others.

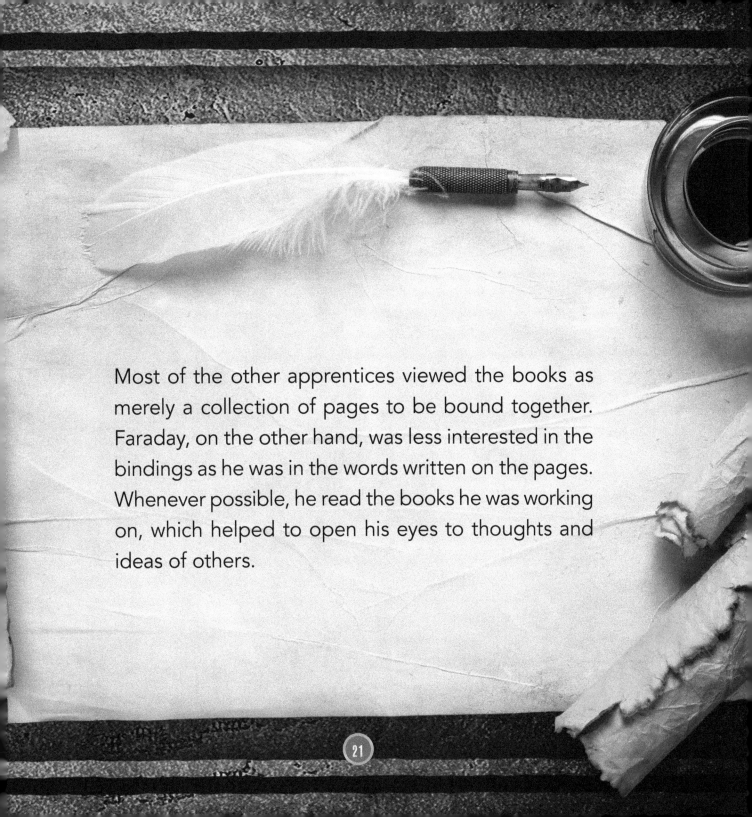

Most of the other apprentices viewed the books as merely a collection of pages to be bound together. Faraday, on the other hand, was less interested in the bindings as he was in the words written on the pages. Whenever possible, he read the books he was working on, which helped to open his eyes to thoughts and ideas of others.

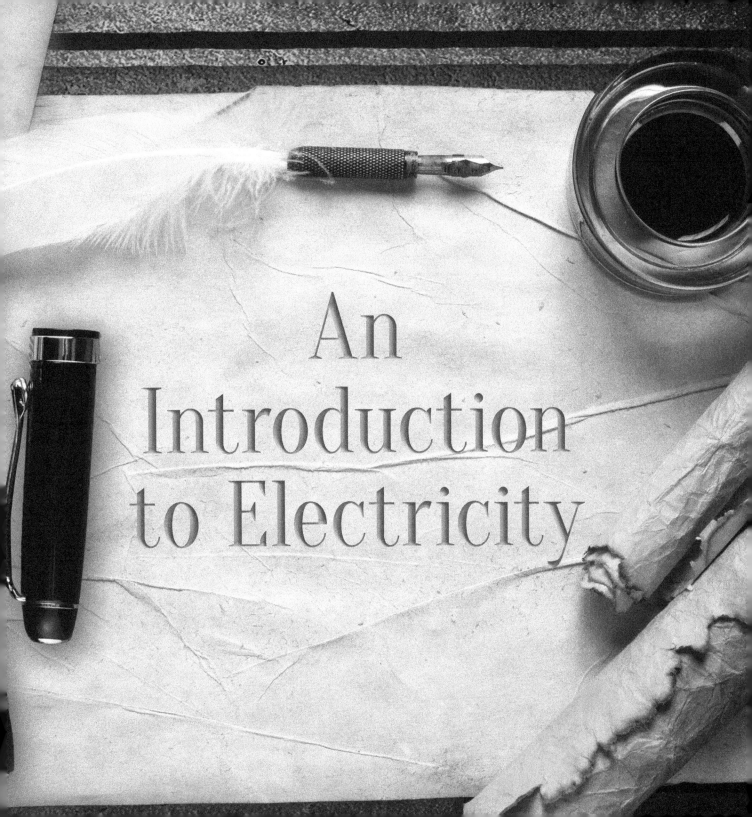

An Introduction to Electricity

It was reading one such book, an edition of the *Encyclopedia Britannica* that a customer was having rebound, that Faraday first read about a fascinating and little-understood phenomenon called electricity.

Encyclopedia Britannica

The article captured Faraday's lifelong interest. He used scrap material to build an electrostatic generator and remedial electric battery and set about conducting his own scientific experiments in electricity. He kept careful journals of his experiments and the observations that he made, but he longed to advance his learning. He finally got his chance.

Michael Faraday's laboratory notebook at the Royal Institution in London.

Faraday and the Scientific Community

Unexpectedly, Michael Faraday was given a pass to attend a lecture at London's Royal Institute. The guest speaker was a chemist named Sir Humphry Davy. At the lecture, Faraday was spellbound. He took careful notes of everything Davy said.

Painting of the Royal Institution of Great Britain, circa 1838, London, England

Although he knew he must return to his job as a book binder in Surrey, he renewed his desire to join the vibrant and growing scientific community in London. Using the skills he learned on the job, Faraday made a bound copy of Davy's lecture notes which he sent to the chemist along with a note inquiring about a job.

Sir Humphry Davy

Davy was impressed with the eager Faraday and offered him a position as a lab assistant as soon as an opening came up. Even though Davy was considered to be a great scientist during his lifetime, most people today say that the greatest thing Davy ever discovered was Michael Faraday.

Humphry Davy was the mentor of Michael Faraday.

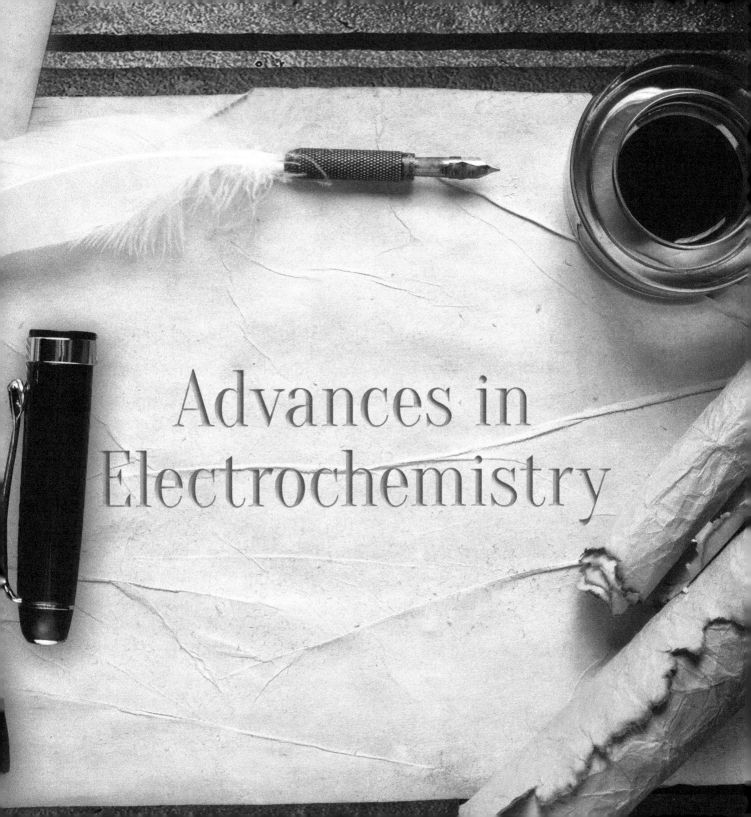

Advances in
Electrochemistry

During the time that Michael Faraday worked for Sir Humphry Davy, Davy was making some tremendous advances in the area of chemistry. It had recently been determined that all matter was composed of unique elements, such as oxygen, carbon, and nitrogen. Davy's experiments led him to conclude that the various elements formed bonds with other elements to create molecules. Faraday's focus on these bonds and how they are held together formed the foundation for his theories about electricity.

Davy giving a chemical lecture at the Surrey Institute.

Ready to Research on His Own

Today, we would consider Michael Faraday to be an amateur scientist because he did not go to college or earn a degree in chemistry or physics, but after working in Davy's lab, Faraday knew more about chemistry than most scientists of his day.

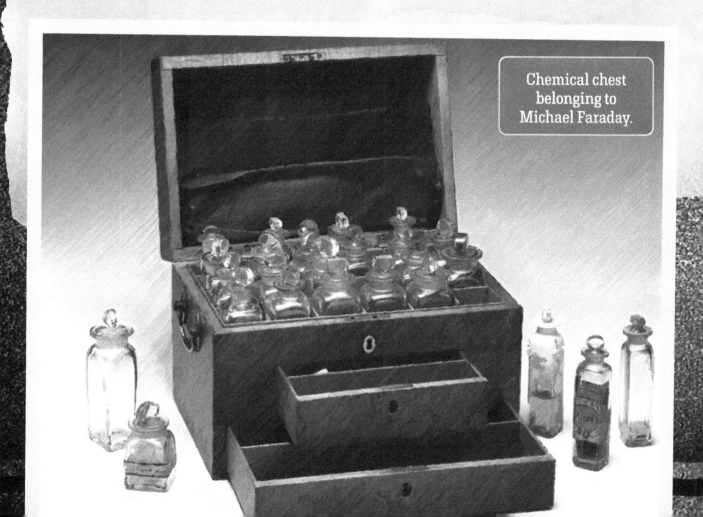

Chemical chest belonging to Michael Faraday.

He had also learned how to conduct scientific experiments, how to record his observations, how to document his results, and how to develop his own scientific theories. Faraday used his theories to guide the research he did on his own and they led him to some of the greatest breakthroughs in the field of electromagnetism.

Michael Faraday conducting scientific experiments in his laboratory at the Royal Institution.

Faraday and Synthetic Compounds

Michael Faraday's theories about the bonds that hold chemical compounds together allowed him to create the first known synthetic[3] – or man-made – compound in 1820. He replaced the hydrogen with chlorine to make these synthetic carbon and chlorine compounds, which was a liquified gas. He was also successful at liquifying other gases.

---

[3] Synthetic – Man-made, or not naturally occurring.

Michael Faraday created the first known synthetic compound in 1820.

Experimenting on coal, Faraday exposed the carbon to heat, light, and other variables which led to his discovery of hydrocarbons. One of these was benzene, derived from crude oil. Benzene is a pleasant smelling, highly flammable liquid that was used to dissolve grease, soothe irritated skin, and to remove the caffeine from coffee beans.

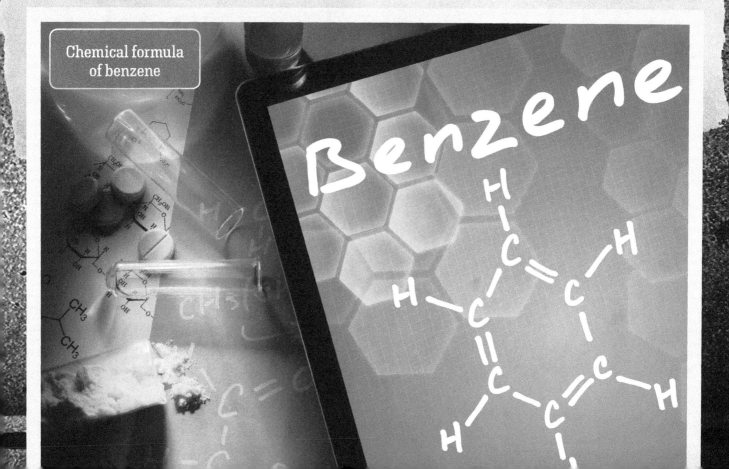

Chemical formula of benzene

Electromagnetism

Despite the work he did in chemistry, Michael Faraday remained interested in electricity. His former mentor, Sir Humphry Davy, was unable to make a working electric motor and he discussed his frustrations with Faraday. Faraday took up the challenge and, using Davy's work as a starting point, created not one, but two, different electric rotation motors. One of his motors was able to sustain continuous motion thanks to a wire wound around a magnet. In his eagerness to publish his findings, Faraday forgot to give credit to Davy in his report. This oversight cast Faraday in a bad light among fellow members of the Royal Society and hung a dark shadow over his friendship with Davy. Faraday did not return to his work in electromagnetism[4] for several years.

---

4   Electromagnetism – The study of electricity and magnetic energies.

Michael Faraday built an electromagnet made of an iron core surrounded by a coil of copper wire.

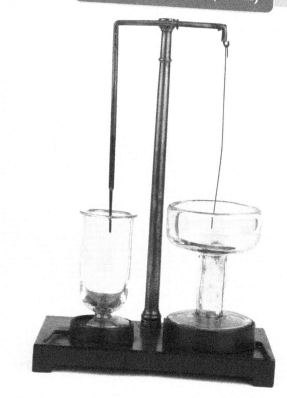

Faraday's electric magnetic rotation apparatus (motor)

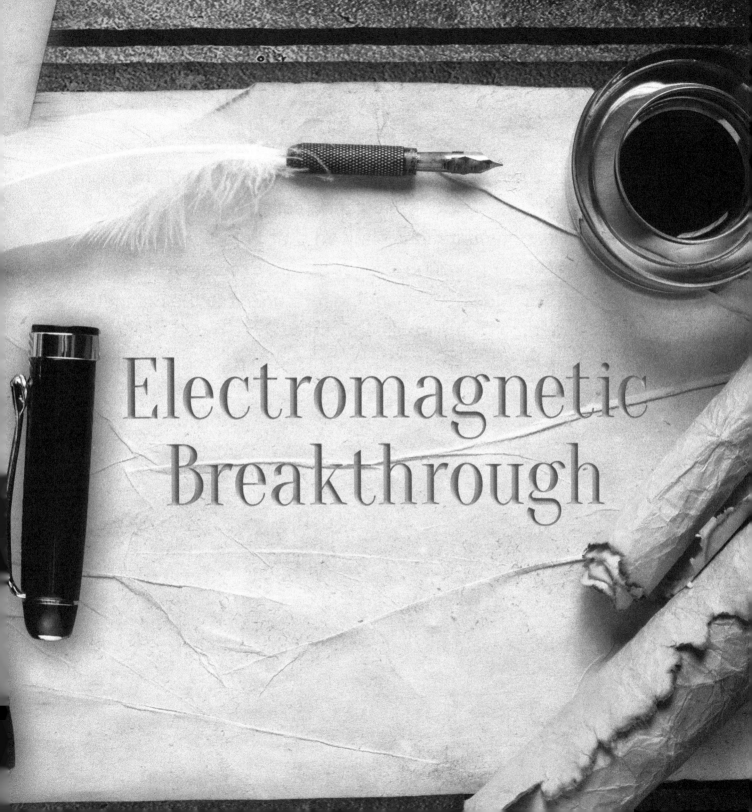

Electromagnetic Breakthrough

Michael Faraday discovered that electrical current[5] could pass from one wire coil wound around an iron ring to another, an action called mutual induction. Further experimentations showed that Faraday could pass electrical current through a series of coils to create a magnetic field. He found that, by changing the current to the magnetic field, he could create an electric field.

---

[5] Current – The flow of electricity.

Faraday's experiment to try to induce a current from a magnetic field using a battery on the left, an iron ring in the center and a galvanometer on the right.

Not only did he demonstrate this phenomenon, but he also proved its existence mathematically in a model known as Faraday's Law. Using the law that was named for him, Michael Faraday pushed his research and experimentations even further, creating the modern electric motor and a forerunner of today's electric generator.

FARADAY'S LAW

Coil of wire

Bar magnet

N   S

Direction of motion for magnet or coil

Faraday's law of induction

Sensitive Ammeter

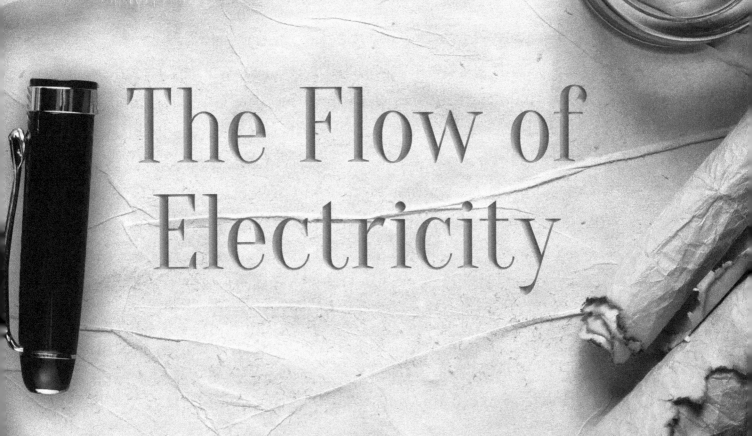

The Flow of
Electricity

Michael Faraday approached the study of electricity from both a scientific and theoretical angle. The hands-on experiments and inventions he built helped him to observe the practical movement of electricity. He also took a philosophical view of the phenomenon of electricity and attempted to understand its nature by thinking outside the box. Here is where his religious upbringing aided his scientific endeavors. Instead of taking the findings of his predecessors as absolute fact, Faraday questioned everything and applied critical thinking skills to research. For example, conventional thoughts of the day stated that electricity was like water that flowed through metal wires instead of through pipes. Faraday, instead, felt that electricity was a force that travelled via vibrations, in a similar manner as sound.

Faraday experimenting on electrolysis in 1833.

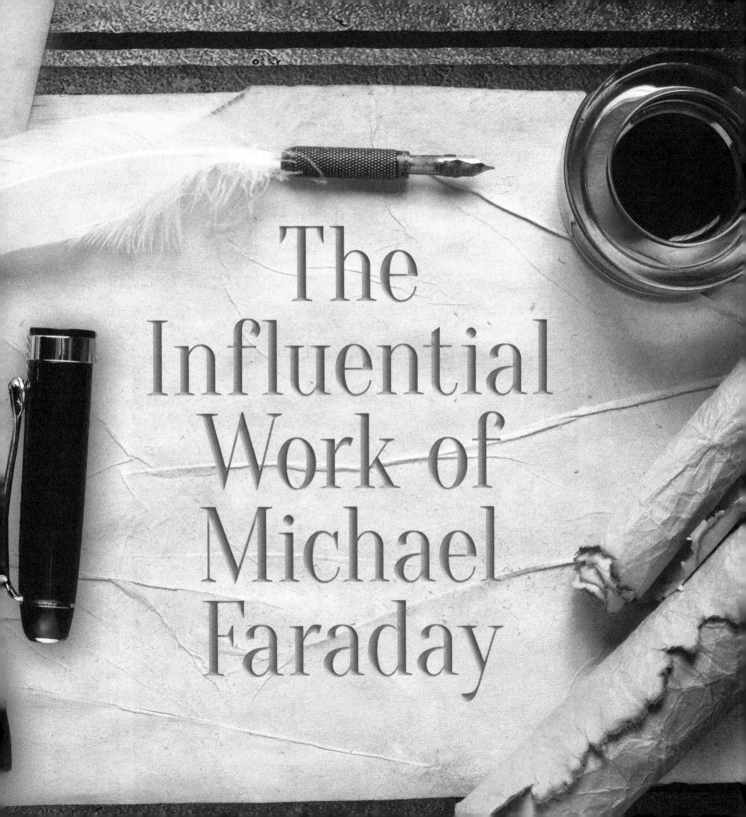

The Influential Work of Michael Faraday

M ichael Faraday's groundbreaking work in chemistry and electromagnetism helped to lay the foundation for the scientific studies that followed. According to legend, the famous German physicist, Albert Einstein, mounted a photograph of Michael Faraday on the wall of his den so he could draw inspiration from the English scientist.

Albert Einstein

Faraday also greatly influenced American inventor and scientist, Thomas Edison, who also experimented with electrical devices.

Thomas Edison

Many other notable scientists, including Sir Isaac Newton, Nikola Tesla, Lord Kelvin, Samuel Morse, Guglielmo Marconi, and Alexander Graham Bell, were either directly influenced by Michael Faraday or drew on his work when doing their own experimentations.

Sir Isaac Newton

Nikola Tesla

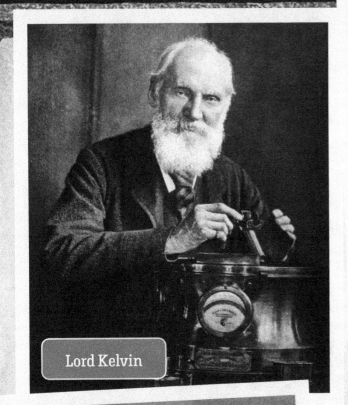

Lord Kelvin

Samuel Morse

Guglielmo Marconi

Alexander Graham Bell

Michael Faraday's Final Years

By the mid-1800s, Michael Faraday was in his early sixties and his once-brilliant mind was beginning to show its age. He drastically cut down on his scientific experimentations although he never fully gave up his life's work. As he fell under the grip of dementia[6], he was not as conscientious with his work. In his senility, he grew frustrated with the Royal Society of London for not publishing his newest scientific papers, even though they were riddled with flaws. Still, his previous work in chemistry and physics was so impressive that Queen Victoria presented him with a cottage and an award to honor his contribution to science. The Queen also wanted to bestow Faraday the title of knight, but he declined the offer, stating that he wanted to be known as Mr. Faraday, not Sir Faraday. He died on August 25, 1867.

---

[6] Dementia – A disease that causes the loss of brain neutrons, leading to memory loss and confusion.

Michael Faraday's grave at Highgate Cemetery, London

MICHAEL FARADAY

BORN 22 SEPTEMBER

1791

DIED 25 AUGUST

1867

SARAH HIS WIFE

BORN 7 JANUARY

1800

DIED 6 JANUARY

1879

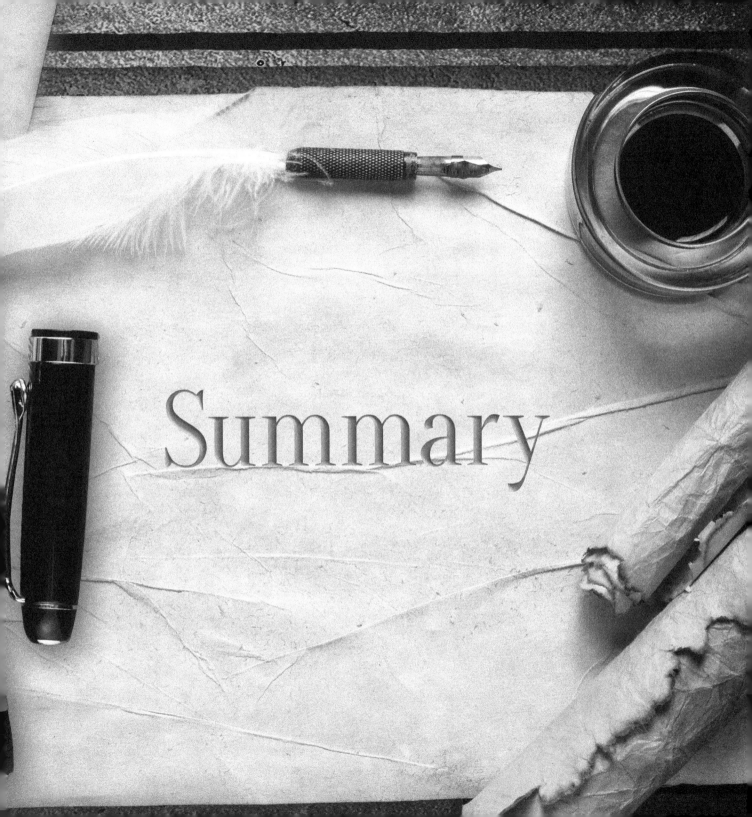

English scientist, Michael Faraday, was a self-taught scientist who became one of the greatest chemists, physicists, and electromagnetism expert in history. He seized opportunities to learn and build on his knowledge and to conduct detailed experiments on electricity, which was an unknown entity in those days.

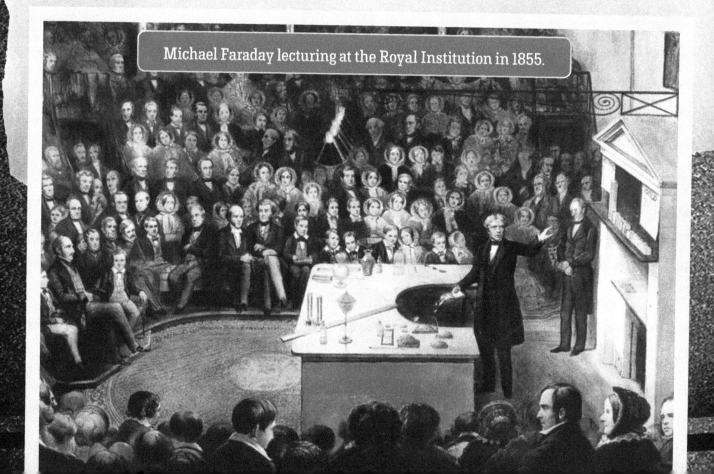

Michael Faraday lecturing at the Royal Institution in 1855.

Michael Faraday was an inspiration to many scientists who came after him, including Thomas Edison, Nikola Tesla, Guglielmo Marconi, and Albert Einstein. The world-changing inventions and discoveries of these scientists may not have been possible if it had not been for the work of Michael Faraday.

Statue of Michael Faraday outside the Institute of Engineering and Technology, London, UK.

SAVOY PLACE WC2
CITY OF WESTMINSTER

FARADAY

MICHAEL FARADAY
SEPTEMBER 22ND 1791
AUGUST 25TH 1867

Now that you know about the life of Michael Faraday, you are ready to learn about some of the other great scientists of the 1800s, such as Alexander Graham Bell, Thomas Edison, and Nikola Tesla.

CPSIA information can be obtained
at www.ICGtesting.com
Printed in the USA
BVHW062059280121
599006BV00005B/302